YOUR KNOWLEDGE HAS VALUE

- We will publish your bachelor's and master's thesis, essays and papers

- Your own eBook and book -
  sold worldwide in all relevant shops

- Earn money with each sale

Upload your text at www.GRIN.com
and publish for free

Mustafa Sezer

Aus der Reihe: e-fellows.net stipendiaten-wissen

e-fellows.net (Hrsg.)

Band 806

From slavery to equality - the development of black people in the USA

Facharbeit

GRIN Verlag

Bibliografische Information der Deutschen Nationalbibliothek:

Die Deutsche Bibliothek verzeichnet diese Publikation in der Deutschen National-
bibliografie; detaillierte bibliografische Daten sind im Internet über http://dnb.d-
nb.de/ abrufbar.

Dieses Werk sowie alle darin enthaltenen einzelnen Beiträge und Abbildungen
sind urheberrechtlich geschützt. Jede Verwertung, die nicht ausdrücklich vom
Urheberrechtsschutz zugelassen ist, bedarf der vorherigen Zustimmung des Verla-
ges. Das gilt insbesondere für Vervielfältigungen, Bearbeitungen, Übersetzungen,
Mikroverfilmungen, Auswertungen durch Datenbanken und für die Einspeicherung
und Verarbeitung in elektronische Systeme. Alle Rechte, auch die des auszugsweisen
Nachdrucks, der fotomechanischen Wiedergabe (einschließlich Mikrokopie) sowie
der Auswertung durch Datenbanken oder ähnliche Einrichtungen, vorbehalten.

Imprint:

Copyright © 2012 GRIN Verlag GmbH
Druck und Bindung: Books on Demand GmbH, Norderstedt Germany
ISBN: 978-3-656-50889-2

This book at GRIN:

http://www.grin.com/en/e-book/262446/from-slavery-to-equality-the-development-
of-black-people-in-the-usa

GRIN - Your knowledge has value

Der GRIN Verlag publiziert seit 1998 wissenschaftliche Arbeiten von Studenten, Hochschullehrern und anderen Akademikern als eBook und gedrucktes Buch. Die Verlagswebsite www.grin.com ist die ideale Plattform zur Veröffentlichung von Hausarbeiten, Abschlussarbeiten, wissenschaftlichen Aufsätzen, Dissertationen und Fachbüchern.

Visit us on the internet:

http://www.grin.com/

http://www.facebook.com/grincom

http://www.twitter.com/grin_com

From slavery to equality - the development of black people in the USA

Facharbeit von

Name	Mustafa Sezer
Schule	Kurt-Tucholsky-Gesamtschule Krefeld
Schuljahr	2011/2012
Fach	Englisch Grundkurs

Table of contents			Page
1.	**Introduction**		3
2.	**History of the Afro-American slavery**		4
	2.1	Its beginning and the situation of the African slaves	4
	2.2	The abolishment of slavery	5
3.	**Literary example of the situation of black people in the 20th century - "Beale Street Blues"**		6
	3.1	Description of the main characters	6
	3.2	The political and social situation of the characters	6
	3.3	Their way out of the problems	8
4.	**Political measures against discrimination**		8
	4.1	Civil-rights activists and their political speeches a) Martin Luther King b) Malcolm X	9
	4.2	Political events	10
5.	**Today's situation**		11
	5.1	Obama's view of today's situation	11
	5.2	Is there still discrimination in the USA?	12
6.	**Concluding remark**		12
7.	**List of literature**		14
8.	**Attachment**		15

1. Introduction

20th January 2009 - The whole world was looking at the USA. For the Americans, especially for the black minority of them, this day was supposed to be a special one, a kind of turning point in the American history. After the presidential elections in 2008, Barack Obama has been sworn to the president of the United States of America. The specialty about him is that he is the first Afro-American president of the USA. As it was an "event" that has astonished people all over the world[1], it is one of the reasons why I would like to write a theory paper about it. It also makes me ask myself the following question: "How is it possible that someone, whose minority has been used as slaves or has been discriminated by white people in the past, becomes the mightiest man of that country?". From this it follows another question: "Who or what has led to it?". These central questions shall attend the entire paper. As you can grasp from the title, I am going to point out the development from slavery to equality in America. This development should be reflected chapter by chapter. Because of the complexity of my topic, it is difficult to write just a 10-page-paper about it and that means I have to limit my work. Therefore, in order to answer the central questions, I subdivide my theory paper into four chapters:

The first chapter deals with the history of the Afro-American slavery in order to give you a short insight into its beginning and into the situation of the slaves. It is also an important topic because Afro-Americans have their origins in Africa.

In the second chapter I will tell you about the situation of black people in the 20th century with the help of a literary example, including their social and political situation. It is clear to me that it is not possible to consider every life of black people in the USA. Because of that, I intend to read and analyze the novel "Beale Street Blues" by James Baldwin where the lives of black people are authentically described. In this chapter I present you the main characters. After that, I will show you how they cope with their given situation and how they try to get out of it.

In the third chapter I will examine how much politicians have contributed to the assimilation of black people in the USA. For that, I will make use of methods like

---

[1] cf. http://www.latimes.com/news/nationworld/world/la-fg-worldreax6-2008nov06,0,6037603,story (11.02.2012)

analyzing speeches of civil-rights activists. Furthermore, I will also focus on important political events and their influence on today.

In the fourth and last chapter I will show how the situation is in the present. Especially, I am going to answer the question whether there is still discrimination of black people in the USA.

2. History of the Afro-American slavery
2.1 Its beginning and the situation of the African slaves

The ancestors of the Afro-American people who are now living in the USA have their origins on the African continent. They had been brought to America in the course of the Afro-American slavery. This slavery started after the discovery of America in the 16th century. At that time, the first African slaves had been brought by Spanish discoverers to the USA[2] whereas the British colonies (13 colonies) had started earlier and they had also contributed to the American slavery. The reasons for bringing and using slaves were, among other things, a huge request of cotton, tobacco, rice, wheat, corn etc. in the USA. Especially there were many workers for cotton because it was one of the main export products of the USA at that time[3]. African slaves had been also employed for the production of their own clothing and nutriment[4]. For today's people, this period is characterized by brutal and inhuman behavior of white people towards black slaves. The following aspects will prove this statement: The whites employed slaves of every age even if they were a child which was usual in the time of slavery[5]. For example, 8-year-old children had to work on plantations[6]. Beyond that, the African slaves had lived in simple cottages without ground floor, without windows and in the rare cases they had a bed[7]. In addition, their workplace were plantations where the slaves worked the whole day until the dawn. Furthermore, they were not able to sleep calmly because they had to get ready for the next working day. In addition, the Afro-American slaves had a lord[8] and a controller who observed them during their work. While doing their job, it was normal for the slaves to be tortured when they did not do their work well.

---

[2] cf. Hubert Feichter, Afroamerikanische Sklaverei - Soziale und wirtschaftliche Aspekte der Sklaverei in den amerikanischen Südstaaten, p. 5, 1. Auflage 2007
[3] cf. Hubert Feichter, see above., p.12, see above
[4] cf. Hubert Feichter, see above., p.11, see above
[5] cf. Frederick Douglass, Mein Leben als Sklave in Amerika, Verlag Lamuv, p. 28
[6] cf. Hubert Feichter, see above, p.10, see above
[7] cf. Hubert Feichter, see above, p.16, see above
[8] cf. Frederick Douglass, Mein Leben als Sklave in Amerika, Verlag Lamuv, p. 24

That means they had been whipped[9] and beaten. Another aspect is that the slaves had been used as if they were products. For instance, they had been sold and hired by slave traders because the white population were in need of them on account of the "cotton empire"[10]. Moreover, many slaves had been fed in a cruel way in order to be more rentable for the acquirer of the slaves. This is an example how brutal the whites had been to the black slaves. During the transportation to the centre of slave exchange, blacks also had to undergo inhuman conditions. For example, they had been tied with chains or handcuffs when they were walking[11]. The last point is that they did not have the possibility to see their family because the family members were separated from each other all the time in most cases.

All in all, one can say that the Afro-American slaves had been treated very inhuman and that they had a difficult time as slaves. For the white population, black people were not more worth than animals in the course of slavery. It is also obviously that their economical profit was more important than the respect towards them.

2.2 The abolishment of slavery

The abolishment of the Afro-American slavery had not been very successful. In spite of the Declaration of Independence from 1776 which should make sure that all men are created equal, I cannot notice any progress concerning the humanity and equality as you can see in chapter 2.1. Especially Frederic Douglass' autobiography shows that there had been still slavery in the 19th century, even after the Declaration of Independence. Nevertheless, slavery has been officially ended. For instance, the Emancipation Proclamation "published" by the American president Abraham Lincoln during the American Civil War (1861-1865) was one of the reasons why Afro-American slavery had been brought to its end. Another point is that slavery had been also abolished in 1865 after Union (the North American states) won the American Civil War against the southern American states. But according to Dietlinde Haug[12], this has not led to the reconciliation between white and black people. Therefore, problems

[9] see 9
[10] Hubert Feichter, see above, p.7, see above
[11] see 11
[12] cf. Frederick Douglass, Mein Leben als Sklave in Amerika, Verlag Lamuv, p. 192

between whites and blacks are also "programmed" for the next years and even for the next century unless there would be a change.

3. Literary example of the situation of black people in the 20th century - "Beale Street Blues"

As you can grasp from chapter 2.2, problems between whites and blacks were not completely solved after Afro-American slavery in the 19th century. That is the reason why this chapter deals with a literary example that is about the situation of black people in the 20th century. The problems which are focused on in the novel "Beale Street Blues" published in 1974 and written by James Baldwin[13] are presented in this chapter.

3.1 Description of the main characters

This novel deals with a relationship between an unmarried black couple. Clementine (Tish), a nineteen-year-old girl and Alonzo (Fonny), a twenty-two-year-old man are in love with each other. At the beginning of the novel, the reader gets to know that Alonzo who is accused of a rape to a Puerto Rican woman in spite of not having done anything is in prison. Meanwhile she longs for her boyfriend Fonny (page 12, "... ich hätte ihn gerne angefasst") and she is proud of him because he can undergo the time in prison. During a visiting time in prison, Clementine has to reveal to Alonzo that she is pregnant whereas Fonny does not seem to be happy (page 11). She can only communicate with him through a glass wall[14]. They know each other since their childhood and they met for the first time when they had an argument (page 18). Clementine and Fonny have lived in the same neighborhood. Before Alonzo had to go to prison, they had had a good time. For example, the couple went out for dinner. Their dreams are among other things to get married and live together (page 63). All in all, Clementine tries her best in order to bring Fonny out of prison.

3.2 The political and social situation of the characters

Chapter 3.1 implies some problems which are caused by the bad situation of the characters. Due to the fact that Fonny is in prison, Clementine will have to care for her child on her own. This makes her very overstressed. In addition, Clementine does not have an apprenticeship (page 71) and she does not have

---

[13] Beale Street Blues, James Baldwin, translated by Nils Thomas Lindquist, Verlag Rowohlt
[14] see blurb

a well-paid job she can sufficiently nourish her family with (page 153). That means she is in a very desperate and bad situation (page 11) and she has to undergo a bad time without Fonny. Moreover, Fonny's job as a sculptor won't help his family. At the beginning of the novel, the reader can also find out that Clementine is very thoughtful about her situation and that she needs some help. Another problem of hers is that she also has to reveal her pregnancy to her parents and to Fonny's parents which is not so easy for her. Particularly, both parents are quite different from each other. Whereas Clementine's parents accept that she is pregnant, Fonny's parents are very upset and curse her baby (page 74) after Clementine has revealed her pregnancy. The reason for this kind of reaction could be that Fonny's parents are very religious and therefore, they cannot accept the baby of unmarried parents. Clementine and Fonny have grown up and also still live in a block in New York which is mostly inhabited by black people (page 16-17). This shows that they prefer to live among blacks instead of getting integrated or even assimilated into the white American society. In addition, they do not fully trust Fonny's lawyer Mr. Hayward because he is white (page 66). Beyond that, Clementine mentions that they have lived or still live in poor conditions. Even her mother Sharon compares their house with a garbage dump in a favela (page 176). Fonny's father Frank has his own establishment and works as a tailor (page 16) and Clementine's father Joseph works at a harbor. Fonny's and Clementine's families do not have enough money, for example they cannot pay Fonny's lawyer or the caution money for his discharge. Before Fonny went to prison, the unmarried couple had looked for a small and simple flat on account of their low salary (page 98).

In the course of the novel, the reader learns that Fonny has been a victim of an intrigue. The person who says that he has seen Fonny running after the criminal act and who arrested him, is a racist policeman who has killed a child in the street. Furthermore, the Puerto Rican woman who has been ostensibly raped by Fonny cannot exactly tell whether he has really raped her (page 173). These are proofs which indicate that there had been inequality towards blacks in the 20th century. Another aspect is that Clementine has been attacked by a white man (page 132) which also shows that there were problems between whites and blacks. In the last part of the novel, the reader gets to know that Fonny has to cope with miserable conditions in prison. On the one hand, he is in a stinking cell and even he stinks (page 170). On the other hand, he has fear to be raped like his friend Daniel (page 166). Fonny's hearing time always changes (page 172) which gives the impression that nobody takes him seriously.

To sum up, you can say that the lives of the black people in the novel are also characterized by social problems like poverty, exclusions and segregation by white people in the 20th century. Nevertheless, Clementine and the others do not give up the hope that Fonny will get out of prison.

3.3 Their way out of the problems

The characters in Baldwin's novel try their best in order to solve the problems mentioned in chapter 3.2. There are different ways how they solve their problems. On the one hand, Fonny's family attempts to hide their social inferiority by going to church and practicing their religion (page 29). On page 29 it is written that Fonny's mother stands straight and that she seems to be aroused and sacred. Apart from that, she wears a pink dress. Compared to other parts of the novel, she has a different, special and especially superior appearance here. In the church she has her own world where there is no problem with whites. Therefore, she can forget her worries. On the other hand, Clementine's mother escaped with a member of her band (page 32) in order to start a new life and to become a singer. But in order to help Fonny out of prison, both families got closer and helped each other. For instance, Frank has accepted that the current situation should be changed (page 181). Beyond that, Ernestine, Clementine's sister, has decided to help her sister by saving money for Fonny's discharge. Another point is that Clementine's mother has gone to Puerto Rica in order to persuade the woman, who accuses Fonny of having raped her, to change her testimony. At the end, Ernestine has enough money to bring Fonny out of prison. In this chapter you can obviously see that cohesion led to solutions and especially to proofs for Fonny's innocence.

4. Political measures against discrimination

This kind of situation the characters of "Beale Street Blues" have to undergo was not an exception in the USA in the middle of the 20th century. Nearly every black people had the same problems which are described in the previous chapter. Politicians, especially black politicians, had the target to change this situation. This change should be achieved by delivering speeches or by events.

4.1 Civil-rights activists and their political speeches

a) Martin Luther King

"I have a dream". That is the name of his famous speech which was delivered at the March on Washington in 1996. In addition, King also uses it as an anaphora in this speech in order to stress his dreams. The problems he mentions are mostly the same problems like in chapter 3.2. These are segregation, poverty, discrimination etc. King also criticizes that Americans did not keep the promise of the Declaration of Independence that "All men are created equal". A characteristic of this speech is that he appeals to blacks as well as to whites by saying that the blacks' destiny is tied up with the destiny of whites. Among other things, King's dreams are brotherhood, freedom and equality. This speech[15] became very famous because it contains an allusion to the roots of the American Dream (e.g. Declaration of Independence). Another point is that it is the one of the most cited speeches (e.g. Obama's speech, cf. chapter 5.1). This speech was also successful because it focuses on problems which were usual for blacks and therefore, King found many followers. In his last speech "Mountain Top" he requests the blacks to stay together instead of fighting against each other because, according to him, it is the way out of slavery. This statement can be verified with the example of the characters of "Beale Street Blues" because their cohesion finally led to the solution of their problems as you can see in chapter 3.3. Apart from that, King is not in favor of violence.

b) Malcolm X[16]

Malcolm X was a member of "Nation of Islam" and a leader of the civil rights movement. In his speech "The ballot or the bullet" he demands equality, including religious equality, and the end of "suffering" from political oppression, from economic exploitation, from social degradation like Martin Luther King. Furthermore, he wants the people to neutralize their differences. That means,

---

[15] See attachment for the speeches mentioned in chapter 4 and 5
[16] cf. http://de.wikipedia.org/wiki/Malcolm_X (19.02.2012)

religion or political attitudes should not play a role anymore. But in contrast to King, Malcolm X criticizes the American system, including its democracy, and he does not seem to be a pacifist. For example, if there is no change of the situation, violence will be used in order to gain civil rights ("The ballot or the bullet"). He is obviously ashamed to be an American. At the end of his speech he calls the "American Dream" as "American Nightmare" in order to describe the political situation. After his death, the Black Panther Party has been founded which set value on Malcolm X's views. This shows how persuasive his speeches were.

In spite of the achievements of both civil-rights activists, King and Malcolm X have been killed by enemies. However, their acts, especially King's acts, had been successful as you will see in chapter 4.2.

4.2 Political events

The civil rights movement have organized several political events in order to fight against segregation and discrimination. One of the most important and effective event was the "March on Washington"[17] in 1963. It was a demonstration for freedom and jobs and more than 200.000 white and black people took part in this demonstration. Beyond that, Martin Luther King delivered his speech "I have a dream" (cf. chapter 4.1). The March on Washington was effective because the Civil Rights Act and Voting Right Act had been passed in 1964 and 1965 as a consequence of that. This is a proof for the success of Martin Luther King's speech, too. Another important measure against segregation was the Montgomery Bus Boycott[18] in 1955 to 1956. The specialty about it is that it was a "direct" act against the segregation in the USA. Rosa Parks was the first person who refused to offer her seat to a white person in a bus. She had been arrested for this behavior. After that, black people came to the decision to boycott this arrest. Within a year black people went by foot and avoided to go by bus until the demands of the blacks were fulfilled. After Martin Luther King's speech concerning the Montgomery Bus Boycott their demands were implemented. For instance, the bus enterprises should have a good behavior towards blacks or black bus driver were also allowed to drive a

---

[17] cf. http://de.wikipedia.org/wiki/Marsch_auf_Washington_f%C3%BCr_Arbeit_und_Freiheit (19.02.2012)
[18] cf. http://www.lebenshaus-alb.de/magazin/003397.html, Artikel verfasst von Michael Schmid (19.02.2012)

bus. In 1956 the bus boycott led to a great success when the segregation in bus became declared as unconstitutional. And for the first time, black people won a nonviolent fight against white people and they could implement the first and one of the essential civil rights which also exists today.

All in all, political events turned out to be very important for the fight against discrimination. In this chapter you can obviously see that political measures led to effective changes for many black people. This was possible because political speeches made people come closer and fight together in order to achieve justice and freedom. After all, black people have accepted that they had to change their miserable situation. In my opinion, the statement from the Declaration of Independence "All men are created equal" became expressed here because of the achievements (Civil Rights ...).

5. Today's situation

40 years after Martin Luther King's death, Barack Obama has been elected to the first Afro-American president of the USA. King's fight for civil rights and equality has made a great contribution to Obama's presidency. Therefore Obama's view to King's acts and the current situation are presented in the following.

5.1 Obama's view of today's situation

As you can read in the introduction of my theory paper, Barack Obama became president in 2009. He delivered a speech called "In Honor of Martin Luther King"[19] where he praises King and points out the things he has done and which effects they have on today. In this speech Obama repeatedly emphasizes King's quotation "Unity is the great need of the hour". Throughout the speech, he tells the listener that deficits (injustice, poverty etc.) should be abolished. According to Obama, the way to unity is not easy and therefore hearts and minds have to be changed. Furthermore, unity has the possibility to bring hope for the things which were impossible before. That is the reason why he sets value on it. Obama also underlines that the pursuit of equality is a matter of every people, not only for blacks. Obama also claims that King's dreams have not been fully fulfilled and that they should be completely achieved in the future. For example, he mentions, among other things, discrimination of homosexual

---

[19] See attachment for the speech

people or in the politics and anti-Semitism, too. Beyond that, Obama admires King for having achieved many things without violence like the March on Washington, his visiting in Memphis or the Montgomery Bus Boycott.

To sum up, you can say that Obama considers King's dreams as the basis of his political reign today. Beyond that, he seems to admire King because he has prepared Obama's way to presidency with his successes like the Civil Rights. Obama also has a huge task because the American people, especially the blacks, rely on him to eliminate the "remaining" discrimination (see above).

5.2 Is there still discrimination in the USA?

According to Christopher Garret[20], the situation of the black people have become better. In contrast to the sixties, black people have more opportunities today. Nowadays there is a middle-class of blacks. The black people belonging to this class have high and leading positions in politics, in culture, in journalism or in education. In addition the economy has increased a lot because of these facts. But one also has to mention that there are still people who are discriminated. These people are mostly from the lower classes. Garret mentions as reason that the Afro-American slavery has still impacts on it. Another point is that the current discrimination is not only against blacks but also against Asian Americans, for instance.

However, you can sum up that there are achievements concerning discrimination in the USA compared to the sixties.

6. Concluding remark

After I have written this theory paper, I came to the conclusion that different aspects led to equality. Referring to my central questions (cf. introduction), I can say that unity or respectively staying together led to changes of the situation of blacks as you can see in chapter 3 or 4. But especially, during or after the sixties there had been a turning point: Black politicians have contributed to the Civil Rights (cf. chapter 4). That is the reason why many black people have high positions in the society now which was not possible before like in the middle of the 20th century (cf. chapter 3). Above all, Civil Rights and the struggle for

---

[20] Political scientist who gave an interview to Deutschlandradio concerning this subject (see attachment)

freedom and equality are the consequences that Obama, a black man, became president. As I have written in chapter 4.2 the statement "All men are created equal" became true, I hypothesize that the success of the political acts is a milestone in the American Dream because it led to the equality that was sought for a couple of centuries. Moreover, you can also say that people, who have been treated as if they were animals in the past (cf. chapter 1), are now one of the most important and significant people in the American society. Nevertheless, discrimination cannot be completely stopped in the USA (cf. 5.2). In my opinion, Obama should "step in King's shoes" and should cope with the current discrimination. In my ending words I conclude that the development from slavery to equality was realized on account of politicians who had the courageousness to recruit a great number of people in order to fight for freedom and equality.

7. List of literature

Books:

Baldwin, James: Beale Street Blues, Reinbek bei Hamburg Mai 1980, Rowohlt Taschenbuch Verlag, ISBN 3-499-14546-4

Douglass, Frederick: Mein Leben als Sklave in Amerika, Göttingen 2006[1], Lamuv Verlag, ISBN 978-3-88977-681-5

Feichter, Hubert: Afroamerikanische Sklaverei - Soziale und wirtschaftliche Aspekte der Sklaverei in den amerikanischen Südstaaten, München 2007[1], Grin Verlag, ISBN 978-3-640-56498-9

Internet:

http://articles.nydailynews.com/2008-11-04/news/17911494_1_fierce-urgency-barack-obama-white-house (11.02.2012)

http://www.latimes.com/news/nationworld/world/la-fg-worldreax6-2008nov06,0,6037603.story (11.02.2012)

http://de.wikipedia.org/wiki/Wikipedia:Hauptseite

1.http://de.wikipedia.org/wiki/Marsch_auf_Washington_für_Arbeit_und_Freiheit (19.02.2012)
2.http://de.wikipedia.org/wiki/Martin_Luther_King (19.02.2012)
3.http://de.wikipedia.org/wiki/Malcolm_X (19.02.2012)

http://www.lebenshaus-alb.de/magazin/003397.html, Artikel verfasst von Michael Schmid (19.02.2012)

8. Attachment

Martin Luther King:
"I have a dream":

[...]In a sense we've come to our nation's capital to cash a check. When the architects of our republic wrote the magnificent words of the Constitution and the Declaration of Independence, they were signing a promissory note to which every American was to fall heir. This note was a promise that all men, yes, black men as well as white men, would be guaranteed the "unalienable Rights" of "Life, Liberty and the pursuit of Happiness." It is obvious today that America has defaulted on this promissory note, insofar as her citizens of color are concerned. Instead of honoring this sacred obligation, America has given the Negro people a bad check, a check which has come back marked "insufficient funds."
[...]
And so even though we face the difficulties of today and tomorrow, I still have a dream. It is a dream deeply rooted in the American dream.
I have a dream that one day this nation will rise up and live out the true meaning of its creed: "We hold these truths to be self-evident, that all men are created equal."
I have a dream that one day on the red hills of Georgia, the sons of former slaves and the sons of former slave owners will be able to sit down together at the table of brotherhood.
I have a dream that one day even the state of Mississippi, a state sweltering with the heat of injustice, sweltering with the heat of oppression, will be transformed into an oasis of freedom and justice.
I have a dream that my four little children will one day live in a nation where they will not be judged by the color of their skin but by the content of their character.
I have a *dream* today!
I have a dream that one day, down in Alabama, with its vicious racists, with its governor having his lips dripping with the words of "interposition" and "nullification" -- one day right there in Alabama little black boys and black girls will be able to join hands with little white boys and white girls as sisters and brothers.
I have a *dream* today!
I have a dream that one day every valley shall be exalted, and every hill and mountain shall be made low, the rough places will be made plain, and the crooked places will be made straight; "and the glory of the Lord shall be revealed and all flesh shall see it together."
This is our hope, and this is the faith that I go back to the South with.
With this faith, we will be able to hew out of the mountain of despair a stone of hope. With this faith, we will be able to transform the jangling discords of our nation into a beautiful symphony of brotherhood.
With this faith, we will be able to work together, to pray together, to struggle together, to go to jail together, to stand up for freedom together, knowing that we will be free one day.
And this will be the day -- this will be the day when all of God's children will be able to sing with new meaning:
My country 'tis of thee, sweet land of liberty, of thee I sing.
Land where my fathers died, land of the Pilgrim's pride,
From every mountainside, let freedom ring!
And if America is to be a great nation, this must become true.
And so let freedom ring from the prodigious hilltops of New Hampshire.
Let freedom ring from the mighty mountains of New York.
Let freedom ring from the heightening Alleghenies of Pennsylvania.
Let freedom ring from the snow-capped Rockies of Colorado.
Let freedom ring from the curvaceous slopes of California.
But not only that:
Let freedom ring from Stone Mountain of Georgia.
Let freedom ring from Lookout Mountain of Tennessee.
Let freedom ring from every hill and molehill of Mississippi.
From every mountainside, let freedom ring.
And when this happens, when we allow freedom ring, when we let it ring from every village and every hamlet, from every state and every city, we will be able to speed up that day when *all* of God's children, black men and white men, Jews and Gentiles, Protestants and Catholics, will be able to join hands and sing in the words of the old Negro spiritual:
Free at last! Free at last!
Thank God Almighty, we are free at last!

(http://www.americanrhetoric.com/speeches/mlkihaveadream.htm; 19.02.2012)

"Mountain Top":

[...]Now, what does all of this mean in this great period of history? It means that we've got to stay together. We've got to stay together and maintain unity. You know, whenever Pharaoh wanted to prolong the period of slavery in Egypt, he had a favorite, favorite formula for doing it. What was that? He kept the slaves fighting among themselves. But whenever the slaves get together, something happens in Pharaoh's court, and he cannot hold the slaves in slavery. When the slaves get together, that's the beginning of getting out of slavery. Now let us maintain unity. [...]

(http://www.americanrhetoric.com/speeches/mlkivebeentothemountaintop.htm; 19.02.2012)

Malcolm X
"The ballot or the bullet":

[1] Mr. Moderator, Brother Lomax, brothers and sisters, friends and enemies: I just can't believe everyone in here is a friend and I don't want to leave anybody out.

The question tonight, as I understand it, is "The Negro Revolt, and Where Do We Go From Here?" or What Next?" In my little humble way of understanding it, it points toward either the ballot or the bullet.

[2] Before we try and explain what is meant by the ballot or the bullet, I would like to clarify something concerning myself. I'm still a Muslim, my religion is still Islam. That's my personal belief. Just as Adam Clayton Powell is a Christian minister who heads the Abyssinian Baptist Church in New York, but at the same time takes part in the political struggles to try and bring about rights to the black people in this country; and Dr. Martin Luther King is a Christian minister down in Atlanta, Georgia, who heads another organization fighting for the civil rights of black people in this country; and Rev. Galamison, I guess you've heard of him, is another Christian minister in New York who has been deeply involved in the school boycotts to eliminate segregated education; well, I myself am a minister, not a Christian minister, but a Muslim minister; and I believe in action on all fronts by whatever means necessary.
[3] Although I'm still a Muslim, I'm not here tonight to discuss my religion. I'm not here to try and change your religion. I'm not here to argue or discuss anything that we differ about, because it's time for us to submerge our differences and realize that it is best for us to first see that we have the same problem, a common problem, a problem that will make you catch hell whether you're a Baptist, or a Methodist, or a Muslim, or a nationalist. Whether you're educated or illiterate, whether you live on the boulevard or in the alley, you're going to catch hell just like I am. We're all in the same boat and we all are going to catch the same hell from the same man. He just happens to be a white man. All of us have suffered here, in this country, political oppression at the hands of the white man, economic exploitation at the hands of the white man, and social degradation at the hands of the white man.
[4] Now in speaking like this, it doesn't mean that we're anti-white, but it does mean we're anti-exploitation, we're anti-degradation, we're anti-oppression. And if the white man doesn't want us to be anti-him, let him stop oppressing and exploiting and degrading us. Whether we are Christians or Muslims or nationalists or agnostics or atheists, we must first learn to forget our differences. If we have differences, let us differ in the closet; when we come out in front, let us not have anything to argue about until we get finished arguing with the man. If the late President Kennedy could get together with Khrushchev and exchange some wheat, we certainly have more in common with each other than Kennedy and Khrushchev had with each other.
[5] If we don't do something real soon, I think you'll have to agree that we're going to be forced either to use the ballot or the bullet. It's one or the other in 1964. It isn't that time is running out -- time has run out! 1964 threatens to be the most explosive year America has ever witnessed. The most explosive year. Why? It's also a political year. It's the year when all of the white politicians will be back in the so-called Negro community jiving you and me for some votes. The year when all of the white political crooks will be right back in your and my community with their false promises, building up our hopes for a letdown, with their trickery and their treachery, with their false promises which they don't intend to keep. As they nourish these dissatisfactions, it can only lead to one thing, an explosion; and now we have the type of black man on the scene in America today -- I'm sorry, Brother Lomax -- who just doesn't intend to turn the other cheek any longer.
[6] Don't let anybody tell you anything about the odds are against you. If they draft you, they send you to Korea and make you face 800 million Chinese. If you can be brave over there, you can be brave right here. These odds aren't as great as those odds. And if you fight here, you will at least know what you're fighting for.
[7] I'm not a politician, not even a student of politics; in fact, I'm not a student of much of anything. I'm not a Democrat, I'm not a Republican, and I don't even consider myself an American. If you and I were Americans, there'd be no problem. Those Hunkies that just got off the boat, they're already Americans; Polacks are already Americans; the Italian refugees are already Americans. Everything that came out of Europe, every blue-eyed thing, is already an American. And as long as you and I have been over here, we aren't Americans yet.
[8] Well, I am one who doesn't believe in deluding myself. I'm not going to sit at your table and watch

you eat, with nothing on my plate, and call myself a diner. Sitting at the table doesn't make you
a diner, unless you eat some of what's on that plate. Being here in America doesn't make you an
American. Being born here in America doesn't make you an American. Why, if birth made you American,
you wouldn't need any legislation, you wouldn't need any amendments to the Constitution, you wouldn't
be faced with civil-rights filibustering in Washington, D.C., right now. They don't have to pass civil-
rights legislation to make a Polack an American.
[9] No, I'm not an American. I'm one of the 22 million black people who are the victims of Americanism.
One of the 22 million black people who are the victims of democracy, nothing but disguised hypocrisy.
So, I'm not standing here speaking to you as an American, or a patriot, or a flag-saluter, or a flag-waver --
no, not I. I'm speaking as a victim of this American system. And I see America through the eyes of the
victim. I don't see any American dream; I see an American nightmare.
[10] These 22 million victims are waking up. Their eyes are coming open.
(http://groups.google.com/group/aus.politics/browse_thread/thread/1b50821be58b490c; 19.02.2012)

Barack Obama
"In honor of Martin L. King":
[...] God had a plan for his people. He told them to stand together and march together around the city, and
on the seventh day he told them that when they heard the sound of the ram's horn, they should speak
with one voice. And at the chosen hour, when the horn sounded and a chorus of voices cried out together,
the mighty walls of Jericho came tumbling down.

There are many lessons to take from this passage, just as there are many lessons to take from this day, just
as there are many memories that fill the space of this church. As I was thinking about which ones we need
to remember at this hour, my mind went back to the very beginning of the modern Civil Rights Era.

Because before Memphis and the mountaintop; before the bridge in Selma and the march on Washington;
before Birmingham and the beatings; the fire hoses and the loss of those four little girls; before there
was King the icon and his magnificent dream, there was King the young preacher and a people who found
themselves suffering under the yoke of oppression.

And on the eve of the bus boycotts in Montgomery, at a time when many were still doubtful about the
possibilities of change, a time whent hose in the black community mistrusted themselves, and at times
mistrusted each other, King inspired with words not of anger, but of an urgency that still speaks to us
today:
"Unity is the great need of the hour" is what King said. Unity is how we shall overcome.

What Dr. King understood is that if just one person chose to walk instead of ride the bus, those walls of
oppression would not be moved. But maybe if a few more walked, the foundation might start to shake. If
a few more women were willing to do what Rosa Parks had done, maybe the cracks would start to show.
If teenagers took freedom rides from North to South, maybe a few bricks would come loose. Maybe if
white folks marched because they had come to understand that their freedom too was at stake in the
impending battle, the wall would begin to sway. And if enough Americans were awakened to the
injustice; if they joined together, North and South, rich and poor, Christian and Jew, then
perhaps that wall would come tumbling down, and justice would flow like water, and righteousness like a
mighty stream.

Unity is the great need of the hour -- the great need of this hour. Not because it sounds pleasant or
because it makes us feel good, but because it's the only way we can overcome the essential deficit that
exists in this country.

I'm not talking about a budget deficit. I'm not talking about a trade deficit. I'm not talking about a deficit
of good ideas or new plans.

I'm talking about a moral deficit. I'm talking about an empathy deficit. I'm taking about an inability to
recognize ourselves in one another; to understand that we are our brother's keeper; we are our
sister's keeper; that, in the words of Dr. King, we are all tied together in a single garment of destiny.

We have an empathy deficit when we're still sending our children down corridors of shame -- schools in
the forgotten corners of America where the color of your skin still affects the content of your
education.

We have a deficit when CEOs are making more in ten minutes than some workers make in ten months; when families lose their homes so that lenders make a profit; when mothers can't afford a doctor when their children get sick.

We have a deficit in this country when there is Scooter Libby justice for some and Jena justice for others; when our children see nooses hanging from a schoolyard tree today, in the present, in the twenty-first century.

We have a deficit when homeless veterans sleep on the streets of our cities; when innocents are slaughtered in the deserts of Darfur; when young Americans serve tour after tour of duty in a war that should've never been authorized and never been waged.

And we have a deficit when it takes a breach in our levees to reveal a breach in our compassion; when it takes a terrible storm to reveal the hungry that God calls on us to feed; the sick He calls on us to care for; the least of these He commands that we treat as our own.

So we have a deficit to close. We have walls -- barriers to justice and equality -- that must come down. And to do this, we know that unity is the great need of this hour.

Unfortunately, all too often when we talk about unity in this country, we've come to believe that it can be purchased on the cheap. We've come to believe that racial reconciliation can come easily -- that it's just a matter of a few ignorant people trapped in the prejudices of the past, and that if the demagogues and those who exploit our racial divisions will simply go away, then all our problems would be solved.

All too often, we seek to ignore the profound institutional barriers that stand in the way of ensuring opportunity for all children, or decent jobs for all people, or health care for those who are sick. We long for unity, but are unwilling to pay the price.

But of course, true unity cannot be so easily won. It starts with a change in attitudes -- a broadening of our minds, and a broadening of our hearts.

It's not easy to stand in somebody else's shoes. It's not easy to see past our differences. We've all encountered this in our own lives. But what makes it even more difficult is that we have a politics in this country that seeks to drive us apart -- that puts up walls between us.

We are told that those who differ from us on a few things are different from us on all things; that our problems are the fault of those who don't think like us or look like us or come from where we do. The welfare queen is taking our tax money. The immigrant is taking our jobs. The believer condemns the non-believer as immoral, and the non-believer chides the believer as intolerant.

For most of this country's history, we in the African-American community have been at the receiving end of man's inhumanity to man. And all of us understand intimately the insidious role that race still sometimes plays -- on the job, in the schools, in our health care system, and in our criminal justice system.

And yet, if we are honest with ourselves, we must admit that none of our hands are entirely clean. If we're honest with ourselves, we'll acknowledge that our own community has not always been true to King's vision of a beloved community.

We have scorned our gay brothers and sisters instead of embracing them. The scourge of anti-Semitism has, at times, revealed itself in our community. For too long, some of us have seen immigrants as competitors for jobs instead of companions in the fight for opportunity.

Every day, our politics fuels and exploits this kind of division across all races and regions; across gender and party. It is played out on television. It is sensationalized by the media. And last week, it even crept into the campaign for President, with charges and counter-charges that served to obscure the issues instead of illuminating the critical choices we face as a nation.

So let us say that on this day of all days, each of us carries with us the task of changing our hearts and minds. The division, the stereotypes, the scape-goating, the ease with which we blame our plight on others -- all of this distracts us from the common challenges we face -- war and poverty; injustice and inequality. We can no longer afford to build ourselves up by tearing someone else down. We can no longer afford to traffic in lies or fear or hate. It is the poison that we must purge from our politics; the wall that we must tear down before the hour grows too late.

Because if Dr. King could love his jailor; if he could call on the faithful who once sat where you do to forgive those who set dogs and fire hoses upon them, then surely we can look past what divides us in our time, and bind up our wounds, and erase the empathy deficit that exists in our hearts.

But if changing our hearts and minds is the first critical step, we cannot stop there. It is not enough to bemoan the plight of poor children in this country and remain unwilling to push our elected officials to provide the resources to fix our schools. It is not enough to decry the disparities of health care and yet allow the insurance companies and the drug companies to block much-needed reforms. It is not enough for us to abhor the costs of a misguided war, and yet allow ourselves to be driven by a politics of fear that sees the threat of attack as way to scare up votes instead of a call to come together around a common effort.

The Scripture tells us that we are judged not just by word, but by deed. And if we are to truly bring about the unity that is so crucial in this time, we must find it within ourselves to act on what we know; to understand that living up to this country's ideals and its possibilities will require great effort and resources; sacrifice and stamina.

And that is what is at stake in the great political debate we are having today. The changes that are needed are not just a matter of tinkering at the edges, and they will not come if politicians simply tell us what we want to hear. All of us will be called upon to make some sacrifice. None of us will be exempt from responsibility. We will have to fight to fix our schools, but we will also have to challenge ourselves to be better parents. We will have to confront the biases in our criminal justice system, but we will also have to acknowledge the deep-seated violence that still resides in our own communities and marshal the will to break its grip.

That is how we will bring about the change we seek. That is how Dr. King led this country through the wilderness. He did it with words -- words that he spoke not just to the children of slaves, but the children of slave owners. Words that inspired not just black but also white; not just the Christian but the Jew; not just the Southerner but also the Northerner.

He led with words, but he also led with deeds. He also led by example. He led by marching and going to jail and suffering threats and being away from his family. He led by taking a stand against a war, knowing full well that it would diminish his popularity. He led by challenging our economic structures, understanding that it would cause discomfort. Dr. King understood that unity cannot be won on the cheap; that we would have to earn it through great effort and determination.

That is the unity -- the hard-earned unity -- that we need right now. It is that effort, and that determination, that can transform blind optimism into hope -- the hope to imagine, and work for, and fight for what seemed impossible before.

[...]

But it is where we begin. It is why the walls in that room began to crack and shake.
And if they can shake in that room, they can shake in Atlanta.
And if they can shake in Atlanta, they can shake in Georgia.
And if they can shake in Georgia, they can shake all across America.
And if enough of our voices join together; we can bring those walls
tumbling down. The walls of Jericho can finally come tumbling down.
That is our hope -- but only if we pray together, and work together,
and march together.
Brothers and sisters, we cannot walk alone.
In the struggle for peace and justice, we cannot walk alone.
In the struggle for opportunity and equality, we cannot walk alone
In the struggle to heal this nation and repair this world, we cannot walk alone.
So I ask you to walk with me, and march with me, and join your voice
with mine, and together we will sing the song that tears down the walls
that divide us, and lift up an America that is truly indivisible, with
liberty, and justice, for all. May God bless the memory of the great

pastor of this church, and may God bless the United States of America.
(http://uswahl2008.de/index.php?/archives/632-Wortwoertlich-Obamas-Martin-Luther-King-Rede.html; 25.02.2012)

"Diskriminierung gibt es immer noch" Interview von Deutschlandfunk

Bettina Klein: Beim Blick auf die Geschichte kann man eines festhalten: Unsere Welt verändert sich nur, weil es Menschen gibt, die daran glauben und die eine Vision davon haben, dass die Zukunft anders, besser aussehen könnte. Sie werden verlacht, verfolgt und manchmal bezahlen sie mit ihrem Leben - so wie vor genau 40 Jahren der schwarze Bürgerrechtler Martin Luther King. Und manchmal, erst Jahrzehnte später bemerkt die Welt, was ihr Traum eigentlich bewirkt hat: zum Beispiel den ersten Präsidentschaftsbewerber mit farbiger Haut und realen Chancen, im Weißen Haus zu regieren. Am 4. April 1968 wurde Martin Luther King ermordet. Wir wollen den Blick auf die Gegenwart richten. Christopher Garret ist Politikwissenschaftler aus den USA. Er arbeitet an der Universität Leipzig und wir sind jetzt mit ihm am Telefon verbunden. Ich grüße Sie, Mr. Garret!

Christopher Garret: Schönen guten Tag!

Bettina: Dass es Fortschritte in Fragen der Gleichberechtigung zwischen Schwarzen und Weißen gegeben hat im Vergleich zu den sechziger Jahren, das ist offensichtlich. Aber wie stark wirken die Klischees, wirken Misstrauen und Benachteiligung heute noch, 40 Jahre nach der Aufhebung der Rassentrennung, 40 Jahre nach Luther Kings Ermordung in den USA?

Garret: Diskriminierung gibt es allerdings immer noch in den USA. Das ist überall zu erfahren. Gerade unter den Schwarzen hört man die Debatte zur Diskriminierung und es wird gesagt, es gibt eine wirklich harte Diskriminierung, wirklich absichtliche Diskriminierung.

Klein: Worin besteht diese Diskriminierung heute?

Garret: Heute redet man eher von sogenannter weicher Diskriminierung. Das heißt, es geht meistens um Sprache, Tendenzen und nicht Förderung von bestimmten Leuten, diese Art von Missverständnis, Leute die wirklich nicht die gleichen Chancen bekommen als andere, manchmal Weiße, aber manchmal auch aus anderen Ecken der Gesellschaft, zum Beispiel asiatische Amerikaner, die schneller nach vorne kommen.

Klein: Aber es gibt auch Förderprogramme. Es gibt die Entstehung einer schwarzen Mittelschicht und es gibt Vorbilder auf höchster politischer Ebene. Also, es muss sich einiges ja verbessert haben?

Garret: Auf alle Fälle! Ich möchte Diskriminierung nicht zu viel betonen im Sinne wie Sie vorhin sagten, die Lage wäre ähnlich wie in den sechziger Jahren. Wir haben wirklich sehr große Schritte gemacht. Sie haben es erwähnt. Die große schwarze Mittelschicht, die immer noch sehr gering wächst. Also, Machtpositionen in der Politik, in der Kultur - in der Kultur geht es nicht nur um Produktion von Kultur, sondern wirklich Führung von Kultur, Machtpositionen in der Gesellschaft insgesamt, bei Zeitungen zum Beispiel, Redakteure - überall in der Gesellschaft, in der Bildung, an Universitäten zum Beispiel, da sehen wir viel mehr schwarze Amerikaner zurzeit, die Machtpositionen haben, als vor 40 Jahren. Und noch einmal, die Wirtschaftskraft hat sich massiv gesteigert.

Wo es wirklich schwierig ist, das ist für diejenigen, die noch nicht in der Mittelschicht sind. Die sind manchmal ausgegrenzt. Das hängt davon ab, wo die wohnen zum Beispiel, Ausbildungsmöglichkeiten immer noch und manche beklagen, sogar diejenigen, die in der Mittelschicht sind: Die kommen wirklich nicht ganz nach vorne, weil da sind die Tendenzen immer noch zu spüren: Weiße Menschen in diesen Positionen befürworten weiße Menschen. Das ist aber sehr schwierig nachzuweisen.

Klein: Einwanderer aus muslimischen Staaten gelten in den Vereinigten Staaten von Amerika als sehr gut integriert, anders als in Deutschland zum Beispiel. Bei der schwarzen Minderheit sieht das immer noch anders aus. Wirkt die Geschichte, die ja auch eine der Sklaverei war, da immer noch nach?

Garret: Die wirkt immer noch nach. Das hörten wir zum Beispiel in der Rede von Barack Obama vor einigen Tagen in Philadelphia zur Rassendiskriminierung, zur Rassenpolitik in den USA. Das ist allerdings der Fall. Also es gibt eine große Debatte innerhalb der schwarzen Gemeinde in den USA, und da sind die Meinungen sehr geteilt. Woran liegt das, dass - wie Sie es erwähnten - zum Beispiel muslimische Amerikaner insgesamt viel schneller integriert sind und nach vorne kommen, zur Mittelschicht gehören? Und nicht nur das!

Unter den Latinos zum Beispiel: Die schnellst wachsende Mittelschicht in den USA sind zurzeit die Latinos. Worauf ist das zurückzuführen? Es gibt einige Thesen, dass zum Beispiel Familiensoziologie da etwa eine große Rolle spielt. Familien sind intakter unter Muslimen in den USA, unter Latinos in den USA. Andere argumentieren, es hat maßgeblich damit zu tun, wo man wohnt. Also, bestimmte Gemeinden sind einfach strukturell benachteiligt. Es gibt also verschiedene Meinungen. Sklaverei spielt immer noch eine große Rolle. Das hat Barack Obama direkt angesprochen in seiner Rede in Philadelphia zum Beispiel.

Klein: Er hat ja bis vor wenigen Tagen, muss man ja fast sagen, versucht, selbst die Rassenfrage aus dem Wahlkampf herauszuhalten. Es ist ihm nicht gelungen, offensichtlich, weil es noch ein Thema war. Besteht die Gefahr, dass er daran noch scheitert?

Garret: Ich denke, wir haben mit dieser Rede ein neues Kapitel in dieser Wahlsaison aufgeschlagen. Das heißt, es nicht mehr zu vermeiden, aber es wird nicht mehr wie vorher diskutiert und debattiert. Das heißt, sein Plädoyer in dieser Rede, viel offener, ohne Klischees, ohne politische Korrektheit über Rassenpolitik zu reden, ich denke dieses Plädoyer ist sehr gut unter den Wählern angekommen und sogar unter den anderen Kandidaten. Wir müssen abwarten, wie das wirklich taktisch weitergeführt wird, zum Beispiel unter den Republikanern: Werden die versuchen, geschickt so ein bisschen weiße Befürctungen gegenüber Schwarzen aufzuheizen? Da müssen wir abwarten. Aber ich denke das Land ist insgesamt sehr dafür bereit, diese Debatte, diese Diskussion, wofür Obama plädiert, wirklich zu halten und durchzuführen.

Klein: Obamas Bekenntnis zum christlichen Glauben und sein starkes Plädoyer für Versöhnung, auch seine eigenen sehr unterschiedlichen Wurzeln in seiner eigenen Familie, das wird alles als charakteristischer Unterschied zu früheren farbigen Bewerbern bezeichnet. Hat er eine Strahlkraft, die auf die heutige Zeit übertragen mit jener von Luther Kings damals vergleichbar ist?

Garret: Ich denke schon. Im Hintergrundbericht, der ausgestrahlt wurde in dieser Sendung, hörte man die Melodie in der Rede von Martin Luther King und das hat Obama auf alle Fälle drauf. Das hört man tagaus, tagein in dieser Campagnen-Saison - bei normalen Veranstaltungen, wo er Reden hält oder einfach mit den Wählern redet. Es gibt diese Melodie. Es gibt diese Verbindung mit den Wählern dadurch und das sehen wir sogar in den Umfragen.

Er kommt deutlich besser bei den Wählern in diesem Sinne an. In der Politik spielt das natürlich eine Rolle. Das sehen wir sogar in Deutschland. Denken wir etwa an den Unterschied zwischen Gerhard Schröder und Edmund Stoiber bei Debatten. Das spielt eine Rolle! Man sollte es nicht zu viel betonen, aber diese Mischung aus Naturtalent in der Rhetorik, an Glaube und der Überzeugungseffekt davon, dann diese Melodie in seinen Reden und dann der Inhalt seiner Politik, das kommt dann alles zusammen.

Klein: Christopher Garret war das, Politikwissenschaftler an der Universität Leipzig. Ich bedanke mich für das Gespräch, Mr. Garret.

Garret: Ich danke Ihnen!

(http://www.dradio.de/dlf/sendungen/interview_dlf/764700/; 25.02.2012)